D1146100

MAIASAURA

by Janet Riehecky
illustrated by Diana Magnuson

THE CHILD'S WORLD

MANKATO, MN

*Grateful appreciation is expressed to Bret S. Beall,
Curatorial Coordinator for the Department of Geology,
Field Museum of Natural History, Chicago, Illinois,
who reviewed this book to insure its accuracy.*

Library of Congress Cataloging in Publication Data

Riehecky, Janet, 1953-
   Maiasaura / by Janet Riehecky ; illustrated by Diana Magnuson.
     p. cm. — (Dinosaurs)
   Summary: Describes the physical characteristics and probable
behavior of the dinosaur whose name means "good mother lizard."
   ISBN 0-89565-543-8
   1. Maiasaura—Juvenile literature.   [1. Maiasaura.
2. Dinosaurs.]   I. Magnuson, Diana, ill.   II. Title   III. Series:
Riehecky, Janet, 1953-   Dinosaur books.
QE862.O65R534   1989
567.9'7—dc20   89-22076
                              CIP
                              AC

3 4 5 6 7 8 9 10 11 12 R 97 96 95 94 93

MAIASAURA

Millions of years ago there weren't any people living on earth—which was a good thing, because there were millions of dino-saurs!

Dinosaurs didn't have an easy life. It took a lot of work to stay alive back then.

Dinosaurs had to work hard to get food.
Some had to chase and catch it.

And some had to sneak in and take it.
(And not get caught!)

Dinosaurs also had to work hard to
defend themselves. They could band to-
gether in a herd . . .

or use a weapon to fight off an attacker.

Several types of dinosaurs even worked hard at raising their babies. Their children had a better chance to survive because they had good mothers. One of these dinosaurs was the Maiasaura (my-uh-SAWR-uh or mah-ee-ah-SAWR-uh), which means "good mother lizard."

Scientists have learned that Maiasaurs carefully made nests, watched over their eggs, and cared for their babies until the babies were old enough to care for themselves.

The Maiasaura was a duck-billed dino-saur. Duck-billed is a nickname given to several different types of dinosaurs that had mouths shaped like a duck's bill. The Maiasaura didn't have any teeth in the front of its long, flat mouth, but in its cheeks, it had hundreds of them.

Many duck-billed dinosaurs had fancy crests on their heads, but the Maiasaura's head was flat, with just a short, bony spike above its eyes. Some scientists think the Maiasaura might have had a flap of skin, like the comb of a rooster, attached to the spike. Male Maiasaurs could have used that to attract the attention of female Maiasaurs.

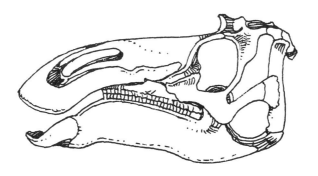

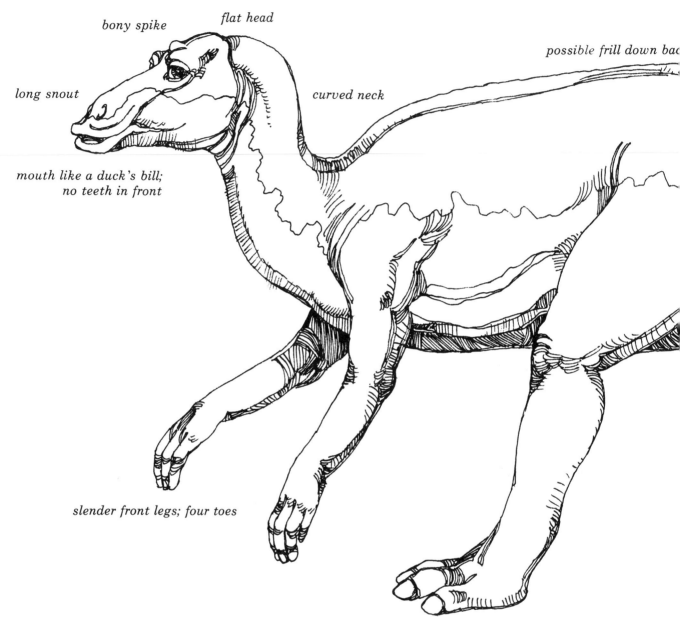

bony spike

flat head

possible frill down bac

long snout

curved neck

mouth like a duck's bill;
no teeth in front

slender front legs; four toes

A Maiasaur was about the size of a camping trailer. That may sound big, but it was only average for a dinosaur. Most adult Maiasaurs grew about twenty-five feet long. A few Maiasaurs grew as long as thirty feet. They stood about fifteen feet high and weighed two or three tons.

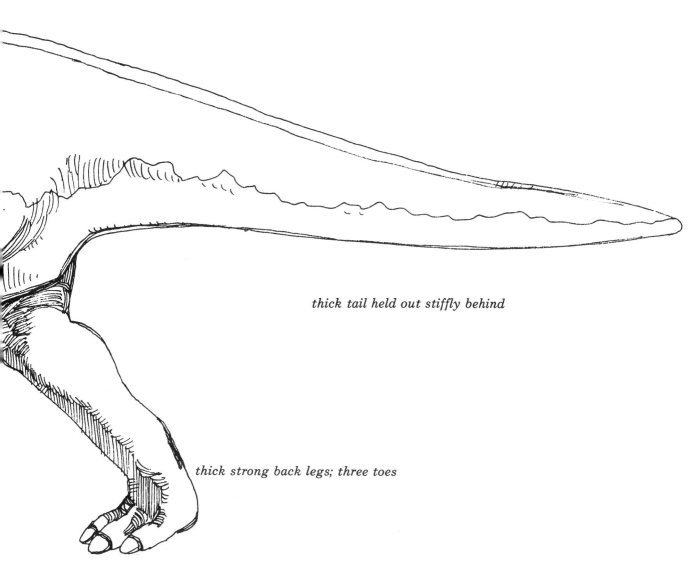

thick tail held out stiffly behind

thick strong back legs; three toes

Maiasaurs walked on their two back
legs. These legs were thick and strong, so
Maiasaurs could run if they needed to.
(And if they saw a Tyrannosaurus, they
would need to!) Their front legs were
smaller and thinner than their back legs
and had four "fingers."

The neck of the Maiasaura was curved like a goose or chicken. As it walked across the land, its head probably bobbed forward and back, like a gigantic bird.

You might expect that a creature that walked like a bird and had a duck's bill would quack like a duck or honk like a goose. And you might be right. Scientists don't know what sound the Maiasaura made—or if it could make any sound at all.

But scientists have discovered that the Maiasaura did have a hollow space in its upper jaw. Air could have been forced through it, like a flute. So the Maiasaura may have filled its world with sound. But whether that sound was a honk or a hum or a quack, we just don't know.

The Maiasaura was a plant-eating dinosaur. It ate tree needles, twigs, seeds, and berries. As you might expect, chewing these tough, woody foods wore its teeth down. But the Maiasaura had an easy way to avoid the dentist. It had teeth stacked inside its jaws, one on top of the other. Whenever a tooth wore out, it just fell out and was replaced by the one underneath it.

Baby Maiasaurs hatched from eggs. The mothers laid the eggs in bowl-shaped nests. As you might guess, these big creatures needed BIG nests! Your mother could probably lie down in one with room to spare.

The "good mother lizards" made their nests very carefully. Scientists think they used their powerful back legs to make a huge mound of dirt on a flat plain and used their arms to hollow out a six-foot-wide bowl in the center of the mound.

Many Maiasaurs made their nests in the same area. The nests were about twenty-three feet apart. This distance was close to the size of an adult Maiasaur. This meant the mothers could wander around and visit each other without stepping on anyone else's nest.

A Maiasaur laid its eggs in a circle. It laid one to two dozen eggs in two layers. The eggs were oval-shaped, about eight inches long, and had a rough, ridged surface. The mother probably brought plants to the nest to cover the eggs to keep them warm. If it had sat on them, it would have squashed them!

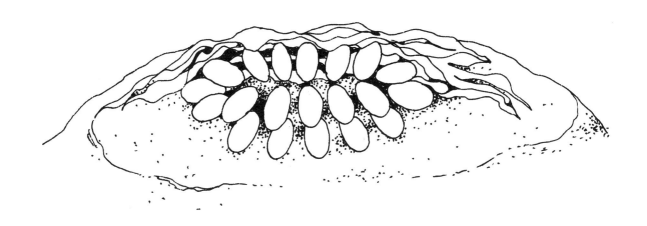

The Maiasaura babies were about fourteen inches long when they were born—about the size of one of their mother's feet. Each weighed only three or four pounds. The mother may have led its babies to a nearby stream to get food. However, it is more likely that the mother brought food to its babies while they stayed in the nest, just as a mother bird will do today.

The babies lived in their nest until they were at least three feet long. That probably took several months. All that time their mother or another adult took care of them. An adult not only brought the babies food but also guarded them from meat-eating dinosaurs, looking for a Maiasaura snack.

In time, the babies grew big enough to join a herd. But they were still given special protection. The little dinosaurs were probably grouped near the middle of the herd with the bigger ones forming a wall of protection around the outside.

Huge herds of Maiasaurs roamed the upper coastal plains—as many as ten thousand in a single herd! They would eat all the plants in one place and then move on to another. Scientists think they may have traveled a regular route, always returning to the same nesting ground when it was time to lay their eggs.

Scientists have learned so much about the Maiasaura because of an amazing discovery made in Montana in 1978 by a man named John R. Horner. Horner and his crew found many dinosaur nests, contain-

ing skeletons of babies. Adult dinosaur bones were found nearby. Horner also found a vast field with the bones of a herd of ten thousand Maiasaurs.

As Horner studied the dinosaur bones and nests, he learned many things about the Maiasaura. He figured out that the babies stayed in the nests after they hatched, because different nests had babies of different ages. The egg shells were all crushed in the bottoms of the nests, as if they had been walked over many times.

Horner also figured out that the babies had been eating, because their teeth were already starting to wear down. Horner and his crew spent several years trying to learn the Maiasaura's secrets. But many things about this dinosaur still remain a puzzle.

Horner and other scientists will continue to study dinosaur finds to learn more about dinosaurs. Finding bones and footprints and dinosaur nests can help us figure out much about these amazing dinosaurs.

Dinosaur Fun

Wouldn't it be exciting to discover a fossilized Maiasaura nest? Imagine how big it would be! But you can do more than imagine. You can find out for yourself. You will need 12-15 pieces of paper, at least 8 inches by 6 inches.

1. Make a pattern for a Maiasaura egg. It should be an oval about 8 inches long.
2. Trace and cut out 12 to 15 eggs.
3. Arrange the eggs in a circle. How big is the group of eggs? How big would a nest have to be to hold those eggs? How would it compare with birds' nests you have seen?